Puppy to Dog

Camilla de la Bédoyère

Words in **bold** are explained in the Glossary on page 22.

Copyright © QED Publishing 2011

First published in the UK in 2011 by
QED Publishing
A Quarto Group company
226 City Road
London EC1V 2TT

www.qed-publishing.co.uk

A catalogue record for this book is available
from the British Library.

ISBN 978 1 84835 582 8

Printed in China

Editor Alexandra Koken
Designer and Picture Researcher Melissa Alaverdy

Picture credits
(t=top, b=bottom, l=left, r=right, c=centre)

Alamy 12 blickwinkel, 14 Juniors Bildarchiv, 16 Simon Hart, 17 Juniors
Bildarchiv

Corbis 6 Herbert Spichtiger, 13 Michael DeYoung

FLPA 1 Mark Raycroft/Minden Pictures, 7r Bernd Brinkmann

NPL 10 Jane Burton, 17 Jane Burton

Photolibrary front cover Stefanie Krause-Wieczorek/Imagebroker.
net, 1t and 8b Phoebe Dunn, 5 Malcom Penny, 15 Justin Paget,
19 Juniors Bildarchiv, 20-21 Edwin Stauner

Shutterstock back cover Jan de Wild, 2l Potapov Alexander, 2r Africa
Studio, 3t Erika Mihaljev, 4-5 Jean Frooms, 6-7 artur gabrysiak, 8t Liliya
Kulianoniak, 9t cynoclub, 9 Eric Isselée, 11 Aleksey Ignatenko, 18 Zocci,
18t Eric Isselée, 19t Perig, 20 Boris Djuranovic, 21t clearviewstock,
22-23 Eric Lam, 24 adomaswillkill, 24br Eric Isselée

Contents

What is a dog?

Dogs are **mammals**.
Mammals have fur
and give birth to
babies, which they
feed with milk.

Dogs are clever and have
a good sense of smell.
Most dogs are **tame**.
They can become pets
and share our homes.

muzzle

⇨ A dog's nose is
called a muzzle.

4

Some dogs live in the wild.
Wolves, foxes and
dingos are wild dogs.

⇩ African wild dogs hunt in groups. A group of dogs is called a pack.

Some dogs are working dogs.
They help people such as police
officers do important jobs.

Breeds of dog

There are lots of different types of dog. Dalmatian, bulldog, Irish setter and poodle are **breeds** of dog.

Some breeds are tall, some breeds are small. Some breeds love to dig, and some breeds love to swim.

⇦ Poodles are clever dogs. They have curly fur.

poodle

dachshund

⇒ The smallest breeds of dog are called toy dogs.

Irish setter

⇐ Irish setters are also called red setters. Their fur is long, silky and red.

Dogs that do not belong to one type, or breed, are called mongrels.

The story of a dog

Baby dogs are called puppies. Newborn puppies are small and weak. They have a lot of growing to do.

They can look like their mother, their father or a mixture of both.

Puppies change as they get older. One day the female dogs will have their own puppies.

2

⇧ This puppy is three weeks old.

1

⇨ Newborn puppies are born with their eyes closed. The eyes will open in a few days.

3

The story of how a puppy changes and grows into a dog is called a **life cycle**.

4

⇧ This puppy is four months old. It has grown a lot.

⇨ Dogs can live for ten or more years. Some breeds live longer than others.

Making friends

Before a female
dog has puppies she
has to **mate** with a
male dog. They
get to know each
other first.

Dogs like to sniff
one another. They
learn a lot about
each other from the
way they smell.

⇧ When dogs meet they
sniff each other.

male

The male and female dogs mate.
The male **fertilizes** tiny eggs
inside the female's body.

female

⇐ Dogs should not
mate until they
are at least
one year old.

A new life begins

The female's eggs must be fertilized before they can grow into puppies.

When a female has got fertilized eggs growing inside her, she is **pregnant**. She will be pregnant for between two and three months.

⇧ This Dalmatian has a large belly. Her puppies are growing inside.

The puppies get food from their mother's body and they grow. Her belly gets bigger.

⇨ Pregnant females can still go for walks, and enjoy their exercise.

13

A time to prepare

As time goes on, the pregnant mother needs more rest. Her puppies are getting bigger, and she eats more food.

The mother finds a dark, quiet corner to sleep. She prepares this place for her puppies.

⇧ The mother needs a soft bed. It needs to be in a warm place.

14

When it is time for the puppies to be born, the mother stops eating and goes to her **den**.

⇐ The mother is tired. Her body must rest before the puppies are born.

15

Puppies are born

The mother gives birth to a group of puppies, called a **litter**. There are about six puppies in most litters.

The puppies are born **deaf**, blind and helpless. The mother washes them with her tongue. She stays with the puppies, feeds them, keeps them warm and protects them.

⇧ This mother has given birth to eight puppies.

⇨ The puppies suck milk from their mother's body. They cannot eat food yet.

The mother has **teats** on her belly. The puppies get milk by sucking on the teats.

⇨ Dalmatian puppies are born with no spots. The spots will show up in a few weeks.

Growing up

When puppies are two weeks old they can hear and see. They sit up and look around.

Soon the puppies will take their first steps. They want to explore the world around them.

Puppies stay with their mothers until they are about ten weeks old. By that time, they can eat proper food and play.

2

1

⇧ When they are old enough, puppies can go to a new home.

⇦ New puppies need their mothers to take care of them.

⇨ Dogs start eating proper food when they are three to four weeks old.

⇩ The puppy has grown up. It is now an adult dog.

3

How dogs live

Puppies grow up quickly. Some dogs become family pets. Other dogs have important jobs to do.

Dogs are clever, and can learn to follow commands. Most dogs enjoy being busy. They need a lot of exercise.

⇧ Golden retrievers can work as assistance dogs. They help people who are blind or deaf.

When they are one year old, most dogs are able to become mothers or fathers. The life cycle begins again.

⇧ Border collies help farmers look after their sheep.

⇩ Huskies are strong dogs. They pull sleds across the snow.

21

Glossary

Breed
A type of dog.

Deaf
Unable to hear.

Den
A quiet place to rest.

Fertilize
When a male fertilizes a female's egg it can grow into a new living thing.

Life cycle
The story of how a living thing grows from birth to death and how it produces young.

Litter
A group of puppies that are born at the same time.

Mammal
Mammals are animals with fur. Mammal mothers feed their young with milk.

Mate
When a male fertilizes a female's egg the dogs are mating.

Pregnant
This is when a mother animal has babies growing inside her.

Tame
Animals that are not wild. They can be pets or farm animals.

Teats
These are special places on a mother's body where a puppy sucks to get milk.

Index

Notes for parents and teachers

 Look through the book and talk about the pictures. Read the captions and ask questions about the things in the photographs that have not been mentioned in the text.

 Use the Internet* to research different breeds of dog. Find ways together to describe the different breeds. Are they tall, small, skinny or large? Look at their colours, the length of their fur and the type of tail they have to identify differences and similarities.

 Puppies need lots of care and attention, just as human babies do. Talk about what babies are able to do for themselves, and what things adults have to do for them. Discover the ways that babies learn to do things for themselves, and how they change as they grow.

 Be prepared for questions about human life cycles. There are plenty of books available for this age group that can help give age-appropriate explanations. Talk about the way human parents prepare for the arrival of their babies.

 Talking about a child's family helps them to link the processes of reproduction and growth to their own circumstances. Drawing simple family trees, showing them photographs of themselves as babies and talking to grandparents are all fun ways to engage young children.